Today's Apostles

Servants that are Leading God's People towards Unity

Dr. Jamie T. Pleasant; Ph.D.

Today's Apostles

Servants that are Leading God's People towards Unity

Dr. Jamie T. Pleasant; Ph.D.

Today's Apostles: Servants that are leading God's People towards Unity

Copyright © 2013 by Dr. Jamie T. Pleasant; Ph.D.

Biblion Publishing LLC

All rights reserved. No portion of this book may be reproduced, stored in a retrieval system or transmitted in any form or by any means — electronic, mechanical, photocopy, recording or other without the prior written authorization of the author — except for a brief quotation in printed reviews.

Unless otherwise indicated, scripture quotations are from the Holy Bible, New International Version.

First Edition / First Printing

ISBN-978-0984374885

Table of Contents

Chapter 1	Do Apostles Exist Today?	15
Chapter 2	God's Order for Church Government	23
Chapter 3	Are the Original Twelve the Only Apostles?	37
Chapter 4	The Foundation and Cornerstone of the Church	49
Chapter 5	False Apostles	55
Appendix	Apostles Mentioned in Scripture and References	62
Epilogue	Final Thoughts from Dr. Jamie Pleasant	63

Today's Apostles

Have you ever wondered if Apostles still exist in today's church? Are the twelve that walked with Christ Jesus during His earthly ministry the only Apostles in the Bible? When it comes to Paul, how did he become an Apostle? What are the requirements for one to become an Apostle? Is there a ranking order of authority in the church? If so, what is the ranking authority of an Apostle? If you want answers to these questions, then this book is for you. Get ready to find out if Apostles exist in today's church.

Dedication

To my daddy, Anthony T. Pleasant, who was a perfect example to me of a real man. To my wife Kimberly (oh, how I love you darling!), my two sons; Christian and Zion, and daughter, Nacara.

To the New Zion Christian Church Family, Catherine LeBlanc, Mr. and Mrs. King David Singleton, Mr. John Preacher (what a great teacher you are), Merv Green (you are still the man!) and William Bell.

Humbly Yours in Christ,

Apostle Jamie T. Pleasant

Getting the most out of "Today's Apostles"

Congratulations on purchasing this book! Get ready to have a better understanding about the office of an apostle in the New Testament church according to scripture. This book includes five powerfully packed chapters about today's Apostles that are placed in God's church. You can use this book for personal growth or group study sessions. ***Send an email with the class size to admin@newzionchristianchurch.org for access to Bible study leader's video and PowerPoint resources.*** All of the scriptures used in this book are from the New International Version Bible Translation (1984) unless otherwise noted.

Chapter 1

Do Apostles Exist Today?

Ephesians 4:11-13 (NIV)
[11] It was he who gave some to be apostles, some to be prophets, some to be evangelists, and some to be pastors and teachers, [12] to prepare God's people for works of service, so that the body of Christ may be built up [13] until we all reach unity in the faith and in the knowledge of the Son of God and become mature, attaining to the whole measure of the fullness of Christ.

We must first examine scripture to see if apostles can even exist today. If we look at Ephesians 4:11, we see that there are five spiritual offices that exist that are commonly referred to as the fivefold ministry gifts that exist in the body of Christ.

Do Apostles Exist Today?

Write them below on each line.

_____

_____

_____

_____

_____

Now that you have written those five spiritual offices above, think about the local church you worship at today. Do they still have teachers that serve by leading Bible study or Sunday school? Do they still have pastors that still serve by preaching sermons on Sunday mornings? Do they still have evangelists that lead outreach programs and spread the gospel of Christ to people outside of the church? Do they still believe in prophets that can minister a revelatory word to members when the Spirit of God moves in a foretelling manner? You should have answered yes to all of these questions. If then, the offices of the teacher, pastor, evangelist and prophet are still a part of the body of Christ and the local church; shouldn't the office of an apostle still be a part of the body of Christ and the local church as well?

According to Ephesians 4:12, why does the body of Christ which comprises the local church still need an apostle, prophet, evangelist pastor and teacher?

_____

_____

_____

You should have answered, *to prepare God's people for works of service.*

Does the body of Christ that comprises the local church still need people to perform works of

Do Apostles Exist Today?

service? Of course it does. Again, who are the ones that are to prepare God's people for works of service? List all five below.

_____

_____

_____

_____

_____

Now, according to Ephesians 4:12, why is the apostle, prophet, evangelist, pastor and teacher preparing God's people for works of service?

_____

_____

_____

Do Apostles Exist Today?

You should have answered, *so that the body of Christ may be built up.*

Does the body of Christ that comprises the local church still need to be built up? Of course it does.

Examine Ephesians 4:13. According to this scripture, how long will these five offices be needed?

_____

_____

_____

_____

You are correct, *until we all reach unity in the faith and in the knowledge of the Son of God and become mature, attaining to the whole measure of the fullness of Christ.*

Do Apostles Exist Today?

Have we all reached unity in the faith yet? Have we all reached unity in the knowledge of the Son of God? Have we all become mature? Have we all attained the whole measure of the fullness of Christ? Of course not! We haven't even come close to achieving any of these things yet. Therefore, do you think we still need the apostle, prophet, evangelist pastor and teacher? Write below.

_____

_____

_____

Does Ephesians 4:11-13 say anywhere that the prophet, evangelist pastor and teacher will always be needed, but the apostle's role will become obsolete? Of course not. Is there any scriptural reference that says that Apostles will cease to exist? Is there any scriptural reference that says that the role of an apostle in the church will not be needed or diminished? The answers to both of these questions are a definitive, no! Therefore, scripture supports the existence of Apostles today.

Do Apostles Exist Today?

Chapter Review

1. Apostles are a part of the five fold ministry gifts.

2. Apostles are here to prepare the people of God for works of service.

3. Apostles are here to help the body of Christ reach unity in the faith.

4. Apostles are here to help the people of God reach unity in the knowledge of Christ.

5. Apostles are here to help the people of God become mature In Christ.

6. Apostles are here to help the people of God attain the whole measure of the fullness of God.

Chapter 2

God's Order for Church Government

1 Corinthians 12:28 (NIV)
28 And in the church God has appointed first of all apostles, second prophets, third teachers, then workers of miracles, also those having gifts of healing, those able to help others, those with gifts of administration, and those speaking in different kinds of tongues.

Scripture teaches us in **1 Corinthians 14:40 (NIV) 40 But everything should be done in a fitting and orderly way.** Let's also take a look at 1 Corinthians 12:28. **28 And in the church God has appointed first of all apostles, second prophets, third teachers, then workers of miracles, also those having gifts of healing,**

those able to help others, those with gifts of administration, and those speaking in different kinds of tongues. Notice the position given to the apostles. What is the apostle's position listed according to this scripture. Write your response below.

You should have written *first*.

Where does the apostle hold this position of being first? Write below.

You should have written, *in the church*.

It is correct to say apostles are the highest-ranking authorities in the church. Please notice that Christ Jesus isn't the highest-ranking person *in the church,* because he is the highest-ranking person *over the church.* Why is Christ Jesus not the

God's Order for Church Government

highest-ranking person in the church? Please write your response below.

_____

_____

That's right; *He is over the church, not in the church.*

Does the church still exist today? Of course it does. Therefore, we have further scriptural truth to show us that the apostle is still needed and exists today. In fact, the apostle holds an important position in the church as apostles are listed as number 1.

Why are the apostles placed first in the church? 1 Corinthians 12:28 says that they reside over the administering of all the other gifts and offices that exist in the body of Christ. In other words, they govern the orderly fashion of worship and church activity. Scripture shows us that the apostles are the foundation of the church and therefore are the keepers of the order of the church according to Christ's blueprint. **Ephesians 2:19-22 (NIV) [19]Consequently, you are no longer foreigners and aliens, but fellow citizens with God's people and members of God's household, [20] <u>built on the foundation of the apostles and prophets,</u> with <u>Christ Jesus himself as the chief cornerstone.</u> [21] In him the whole building is joined together and rises to become a holy temple in the Lord. [22] And in him you too are being built together to become a dwelling in which God lives by his Spirit.**

Notice the consistency in the ranking of the apostle and the prophet in Ephesians 2:19-22, 1 Corinthians 12:28 and Ephesians 4:11-13. They are ranked first and second in every scripture reference. The reason the apostle is ranked first over the New Testament prophet is that the prophet must be subjected to the apostle based on

God's Order for Church Government

the church government given by Christ directly to them through the appointment of Peter and the New Testament church.

In addition, notice in verse 19 of 1 Corinthians that Paul is giving instructions about church government and order for the members that belong to God's body. Paul is showing us in scripture that we are now part of God's citizenship. In God's kingdom, there are rules, regulations and governmental authority that must be followed. Finally, notice that in Ephesians 2:21-22, that God's household is being built. Again, this is consistent with scripture found in Ephesians 4:11-13 where apostles are shown to be needed until the body of Christ is built up into the unity of the faith and knowledge of Christ by being joined together. When you became a believer of Christ Jesus, what do you become a member of? Write your answer below.

God's Order for Church Government

You should have written, *a fellow citizen with God's people and members of God's household.*

How was God's household built? Write your answer below.

_____

_____

You should have written, *on the foundation of the apostles and prophets.*

Again, according to scripture, how do you rank the offices of the apostle and the prophet?

_____

Your answer should be *Apostle is first. Prophet is second.*

Ephesians 3:4-6 (NIV) 4 In reading this, then, you will be able to understand my insight into the mystery of Christ, 5 which was not made

known to men in other generations as it <u>has now been revealed by the Spirit to God's holy apostles and prophets.</u> ⁶ This mystery is that through the gospel the Gentiles are heirs together with Israel, members together of one body, and sharers together in the promise in Christ Jesus. Notice again how Ephesians 2:19-22, 1 Corinthians 12:28, Ephesians 4:11-13 and Ephesians 3:4-6 all list the apostle first and prophet second. Verse 4 of Ephesians 3 shows us that the mystery of Christ was not made known to previous generations but is now revealed how? Answer below.

_____

_____

You should have written *by the Spirit to God's holy apostles and prophets.*

Please note that it is the movement of the Holy Spirit on the holy apostles and prophets that reveal this mystery. What is the mystery that the holy apostles and prophets are responsible for communicating to God's people? Write your response below.

_____

_____

_____

_____

That is right, *that through the gospel the Gentiles are heirs together with Israel, members together of one body, and sharers together in the promise in Christ Jesus.*

The holy apostles and prophets have been commissioned to teach all of God's people about the unity that exists among the Gentiles and

Israelites. Apostles and prophets must make sure they communicate a consistent message that Gentiles are heirs of the promise along with the Israelites and form one body in Christ. Again, notice this is in-line with Ephesians 4:11-13 that shows the reason there is a need for apostles today. The government that Christ is establishing can't operate in proper order without the apostles and prophets carrying out their responsibilities to solve the mystery of Christ to the churches.

There is no government that doesn't have a ranking system for its officers. In America, the President of the United States is the highest ranking officer over the armed forces. In fact, the United States Constitution names the President of the United States the Commander-in-Chief of the entire U.S. armed forces. If we were to examine the Army, the next highest ranked persons would be the General, Lieutenant General, Major General and so on until we would reach the lowest ranking person, the Private. This ranking and authority is crucial in establishing who has the ultimate command and rights to do certain things. The Private can't tell the General what to do. The General can't tell the President what to do. Each lower ranked person would be out of order and the entire military would be in disarray. The same exist in the Kingdom of God and His government. Christ Jesus heads his government on earth. Apostles are next in command and so forth through church order. The same way we have to obey local, state and federal officers, we must do the same in the body of Christ and the church. **Hebrews 13:17 (NIV) [17] Obey your leaders and submit to their authority. They keep watch over you as men who must give an account. Obey them so that their work will be a joy, not a burden, for that would be of no advantage to you.** We see in scripture that Paul is telling all believers that they must obey the leaders that have been placed over them in church. Not only are we

God's Order for Church Government

to obey to them, we must submit to them. That means, we will have to do things sometimes that we may not fully understand, but trust God it is the right thing based on scriptural evidence. In Hebrews 13:17, what are one of the leader's main responsibilities? Write below.

_____

_____

You should have written, *to keep watch over you*.

Notice also that in verse 17, they must give an account to higher authorities within the Body of Christ about your behavior and their ability to grow you into becoming one with Christ, His Body and the church. How are we to bring joy to the authority place over us in the Body of Christ? Write below.

_____

That's right, we must be *obedient*.

Obedience is the only way those placed over us will experience joy and give a good report about us to God, Jesus and other authorities in the Body of Christ at various levels. The scripture goes on to show that if we are not obedient and submissive, it will be to our disadvantage.

Chapter Review

1. The apostle is the highest-ranking person *in the church.*

2. Christ Jesus is the highest-ranking person *over the church.*

3. The prophet is the second highest-ranking person *in the church* after the apostle and Christ Jesus who is over the church.

4. God's kingdom is governed by the authority of the apostles, prophets, pastors, teachers, elders etc.

5. We must find out what the line of authority in our local church is and adhere to it.

6. Those in authority must give an account to those of higher authority on how we are doing under their leadership.

God's Order for Church Government

7. We always want those in authority over us to experience continual joy.

8. We will always want those in authority of us to give a positive report about us by being OBEDIENT.

9. When we aren't obedient, those in authority over us will not experience joy and it will be to our disadvantage.

Chapter 3

Are the Original Twelve the Only Apostles?

Matthew 10:2-4 (NIV)
² These are the names of the twelve apostles: first, Simon (who is called Peter) and his brother Andrew; James son of Zebedee, and his brother John; ³ Philip and Bartholomew; Thomas and Matthew the tax collector; James son of Alphaeus, and Thaddaeus; ⁴ Simon the Zealot and Judas Iscariot, who betrayed him.

Write below the names of the twelve apostles that served beside Christ Jesus during His earthly ministry before His resurrection.

_____

_____

Are the Original Twelve the Only Apostles?

_____

_____

_____

_____

You should have written, *Peter, Andrew, James, John, Philip, Bartholomew, Thomas, Matthew, James, Thaddaeus, Simon and Judas Iscariot.*

Very often, you will hear people say that an apostle can only be someone that walked with Christ Jesus during His earthly ministry. You will often hear them say that after the original Twelve, there were never any other apostles. Let's see if that is true. **Galatians 1:1-2 (NIV) says,** [1] **<u>Paul, an apostle</u>--sent not from men nor by man, but by Jesus Christ and God the Father, who raised him from the dead--**[2] **and all the brothers with me, To the churches in Galatia:** Paul is one that did not serve with Christ Jesus during his earthly

Are the Original Twelve the Only Apostles?

ministry, yet he becomes an apostle. In fact, during Christ Jesus' earthly ministry, he persecuted the church and killed those that loved Christ. He is known in the Bible as Saul before he experiences his conversion on the road to Damascus. Examine scriptural evidence below:

1 Corinthians 15:9 (NIV)
⁹ For I am the <u>least of the apostles</u> and do not even deserve to be called an apostle, because <u>I persecuted the church of God.</u>

Acts 7:58-59 (NIV)
⁵⁸ ...dragged him out of the city and began to stone him. Meanwhile, the witnesses laid their clothes at the feet of a young man named Saul. ⁵⁹ While they were stoning him, Stephen prayed, "Lord Jesus, receive my spirit."

Acts 8:3
(NIV) shows; ³ But Saul began to destroy the church. Going from house to house, he dragged off men and women and put them in prison.

Are the Original Twelve the Only Apostles?

Acts 9:1-2 (NIV)
¹Meanwhile, Saul was still breathing out murderous threats against the Lord's disciples. He went to the high priest ² and asked him for letters to the synagogues in Damascus, so that if he found any there who belonged to the Way, whether men or women, he might take them as prisoners to Jerusalem.

Acts 9:3-6 (NIV)
³ As he neared Damascus on his journey, suddenly a light from heaven flashed around him. ⁴ He fell to the ground and heard a voice say to him, "Saul, Saul, why do you persecute me?" ⁵ "Who are you, Lord?" Saul asked. "I am Jesus, whom you are persecuting," he replied. ⁶ "Now get up and go into the city, and you will be told what you must do."

We see clearly according to scripture that Paul becomes an apostle but didn't walk with Christ Jesus during His earthly ministry. Consequently, he was against Christ Jesus' ministry. We also see that he is not one of the original twelve apostles. Write below the name of the person that did not serve with Christ Jesus during His earthly ministry but became an apostle.

Are the Original Twelve the Only Apostles?

You should have written the name *Paul*.

There are many that agree that Paul didn't serve with Christ Jesus, but that he saw Jesus at his conversion to Christianity and that qualifies him as an apostle. **1 Corinthians 9:1-2 (NIV) says;** **¹ Am I not free? Am I not an apostle? <u>Have I not seen Jesus our Lord?</u> Are you not the result of my work in the Lord? ² <u>Even though I may not be an apostle to others,</u> surely I am to you! For you are the seal of my apostleship in the Lord**.

Here, Paul is giving a recount of his conversion to Christianity that took place on the road to Damascus. The question then becomes, must one see Christ Jesus in order to become an apostle? If this is the requirement to become an apostle after the original twelve, scripture should clearly state such truth. In verse 2, we see he even

Are the Original Twelve the Only Apostles?

has to defend his apostleship because many are still afraid of him from his days of persecuting the church.

Let's examine **Acts 14:14 (NIV) ¹⁴ But when <u>the apostles Barnabas and Paul</u> heard of this, they tore their clothes and rushed out into the crowd, shouting:** Here we see two apostles listed. List the two apostles' names below.

_____

Yes! *Paul and Barnabas* are listed as apostles. There is no place in scripture that says that Barnabas ever walked with Christ when He was on earth or saw him afterward. **Galatians 1:19 (NIV) ¹⁹ I saw none of the other apostles--only James, the Lord's brother.** Here Paul gives an account of seeing James, the Lord's brother whom should not be confused with the James listed in the original twelve.

Are the Original Twelve the Only Apostles?

Romans 16:7 (NIV) says; ⁷ Greet <u>Andronicus and Junias,</u> my relatives who have been in prison with me. They are <u>outstanding among the apostles,</u> and they were in Christ before I was. Here Paul lists Andonicous and Junias as not just apostles, but outstanding among them. Interestingly, *Junias is the first named female apostle in the Bible.* If Deborah can be a judge and prophetess (Judges 4:4) who was in charge of all of Israel, surely a female can be an apostle as well. Now we must look at a scripture that shows that there were many other apostles ordained by Christ to continue His work on earth other than the twelve, Paul and others mentioned by name. **1 Corinthians 15:3-8 (NIV) says;** ³ For what I received I passed on to you as of first importance: that Christ died for our sins according to the Scriptures, ⁴ that he was buried, that he was raised on the third day according to the Scriptures, ⁵ and that he appeared to Peter, and <u>then to the Twelve.</u> ⁶

Are the Original Twelve the Only Apostles?

After that, he appeared to more than five hundred of the brothers at the same time, most of whom are still living, though some have fallen asleep. ⁷ Then he appeared to James, <u>then to all the apostles,</u> ⁸ and last of all he appeared to me also, as to one abnormally born. <u>Notice here that Christ Jesus appeared to an unknown number of apostles after appearing to the original twelve.</u> This scripture shows us that Christ Jesus appeared to many other apostles that are not listed by name in the Bible. Are you ready for this one? Well, last but definitely not least; Christ Jesus is listed in scripture as an Apostle. **Hebrews 3:1 (NIV)** ¹ **Therefore, holy brothers, who share in the heavenly calling, fix your thoughts on <u>Jesus, the apostle</u> and high priest whom we confess.**

Write below the first title Jesus is given in Hebrews 3:1.

Are the Original Twelve the Only Apostles?

Yes. He is listed as an *apostle*. Also notice that the ranking of His title is first, an Apostle and secondly, a High Priest.

Is there a scripture in the Bible that says when apostles will cease to exist? No, there isn't. There are however, many scriptures that we have looked at in this book that proves that they are still needed in order for the body of Christ to function properly.

If we carefully examine the definition of the word apostle, we will find it comes from the Greek word apostello; which means to be a **delegate**; specially an **ambassador** of the Gospel; officially a **commissioner** of Christ ["**apostle**"] (with miraculous powers) :- apostle, messenger, he that is sent. It is clear from examining this definition from the original Greek language that the existence and necessity of an apostle is key to the maturing of the body of Christ. Remember to always examine scripture for the truth of God.

Are the Original Twelve the Only Apostles?

The word of God will always answer any questions one could have about anything concerning the order of the present day church. Let the scripture below guide you to a place of truth, peace and fulfillment in Christ.

Ephesians 4:11-13 (NIV) [11] It was he who gave <u>some to be apostles,</u> some to be prophets, some to be evangelists, and some to be pastors and teachers, [12] <u>to prepare</u> God's people for works of service, so that the body of Christ may be built up [13] <u>until we all reach unity</u> in the faith and in the knowledge of the Son of God <u>and become mature</u>, attaining to the <u>whole measure of the fullness of Christ.</u> We are definitely not there yet, but are on our way. We should thank God for the presence of modern day apostles of Christ in the church.

Are the Original Twelve the Only Apostles?

Chapter Review

1. The original twelve are not the only apostles mentioned in the Bible.

2. The definition of apostle means to be a **delegate**; specially an **ambassador** of the Gospel; officially a **commissioner** of Christ ["**apostle**"] (with miraculous powers) :- apostle, messenger, he that is sent.

3. Barnabas was an apostle that scripture never says saw Jesus or walked with him during His earthly ministry.

4. The Bible shows that there are an unknown number of apostles that Christ Jesus showed Himself to after the resurrection.

5. The Bible never says anywhere that apostles will cease to exist.

6. Christ Jesus is listed in the Bible as an Apostle.

Are the Original Twelve the Only Apostles?

Chapter 4

The Foundation and Cornerstone of the Church

Ephesians 2:19-20(NIV)
...God's household, [20] <u>built on the foundation of the apostles and prophets,</u> with <u>Christ Jesus himself as the chief cornerstone.</u>

According to this scripture, God's household is built on the foundation of whom? Write your answers below.

_____

_____

Yes! *The foundation of God's household is built on the apostles and prophets with Christ Jesus as the cornerstone.*

The Foundation and Cornerstone of the Church

Let's take a moment and examine this truth. I have had two homes built in the past. The very first thing that I saw the construction workers do each time was to lay down the foundation. There is no way they could have raised up walls on the house or constructed any other part of the house if there was not a solid foundation. In fact, the foundation of any home built is of solid concrete so that it is strong enough to not be destroyed by wind or storm. Simply stated, if there is no foundation, a house can't be built or stand firmly. Well, the same way my homes were built on a solid foundation of concrete, God's house that is his Church and members of His Body are built the same way. If apostles, prophets and Christ Jesus are not a part of today's church, there can't be any physical or spiritual building taking place among the members of His Body. How can a church be built if there is no foundation? Most churches have a place for Christ Jesus in their services, but very few see any use for an apostle

The Foundation and Cornerstone of the Church

and prophet. What type of church are you worshipping in? Is the house built on a solid, Biblical foundation? On the other hand, is it built on the traditions of man? Are you in a vibrant church where miracles, signs, wonders and the word is being preached with power to transform lives? On the other hand, is it just a great place with very good music that you love to attend because you can get in and out of service in a very fast time? No wonder God's household has no strength these days. There is no strength in the church because there is no foundation. There is no strength in the church these days because there are no solid beliefs in the power of God. There is no strength in today's church because there is no boldness coming from the leaders of the church because their foundation is based on how many members they can keep so the bills can keep getting paid. Apostles and Prophets will always speak boldly whatever God tells them to speak because their foundation is based on Christ Jesus

The Foundation and Cornerstone of the Church

and His gospel. Sometimes that gospel is easy to digest and sometimes it is not. It doesn't matter to the Apostle and Prophet. Their strength comes from the Lord who they know will provide and bless His people regardless of how the message is received.

Also, notice that Christ Jesus is the most important part of the foundation of the church. Ephesians 2:19-20 **...God's household, [20] built on the foundation of the apostles and prophets, with Christ Jesus himself as the chief cornerstone.** According to scripture, what part of God's household is Christ Jesus? Write below.

_____

You should have written *the chief cornerstone within the foundation*. Now let's examine what a cornerstone is. According to The International Standard Bible Encyclopedia, a cornerstone is defined as *the **foundation-stone** upon which the*

The Foundation and Cornerstone of the Church

*structure rested or the **topmost** or **cap-stone**, which linked the last tier together.* Notice how Christ Jesus serves as Alpha and Omega (top and bottom/first and last) in the church's structure. From here, we can see that the apostles and prophets are to rest on the strength of Christ Jesus. In other words, their doctrine of teachings is always based on the truth of scripture according to Christ Jesus. Notice also, that Christ Jesus, the cornerstone is the topmost, cap-stone and extends all the way to the base of the foundation. In other words, Christ Jesus joins the bottom of the foundation with the top of the building. Apostles and Prophets will always be connected to Christ Jesus in order to construct a strong and vibrant household of believers in the Body of Christ.

The Foundation and Cornerstone of the Church

Chapter Review

1. God's household is built on the foundation of Christ Jesus, the apostles and prophets.

2. Christ Jesus is the cornerstone (capstone, foundation stone, chief-stone) of the foundation that joins the building from top to bottom.

3. The apostles and prophets are parts of the foundation that stays connected to Christ Jesus throughout the entire building.

4. There can't be a physical or spiritual church building without the foundation of the apostles, prophets and Christ Jesus.

Chapter 5

False Apostles

2 Corinthians 11:4-5 (NIV)
⁴ For if someone comes to you and preaches a Jesus other than the Jesus we preached, or if you receive a different spirit from the one you received, or a different gospel from the one you accepted, you put up with it easily enough. ⁵ But I do not think I am in the least inferior to those "super-apostles."

The Apostle Paul addresses the church of Corinth concerning false apostles. He states that there are ways to easily identify a false apostle. List them below.

_____

_____

_____

_____

_____

False Apostles

You should have written, *they preach a Jesus other than the Jesus the Apostles preached according to scripture, they release a different spirit then what the Apostles released to the people, they teach a different gospel from the one they accepted, and finally they speak very eloquently, but distort the truth of the word of God.* In other words, the things false apostles say may sound great but they are not in agreement with scripture.

False apostles will try to distort the divinity and humanity of Christ Jesus. They will even teach that Christ Jesus never died on the cross or came from heaven. They may teach that Christ Jesus was just a prophet, but not the one and only Son of God that was born of the Virgin Mary.

False apostles will begin to teach in such a way that they distort the spirit of who God is. They might teach that Jesus never came in the flesh. They might teach that the Holy Spirit is not

False Apostles

a person but just an impersonal force of God. They might teach that the Holy Spirit is not the third person of the triune God.

False apostles might teach that salvation is not free and given by grace but something that you must work for. They might teach that no one will ever know if they are saved until they are judged after the second coming of Christ. False apostles might even teach that you can possibly lose your salvation after you confess Christ Jesus as your Lord and Savior. They might teach that Christ Jesus was never resurrected from the dead. They might teach that Christ Jesus never died for the forgiveness of our sins. They might even teach that you can never be forgiven for sins. All of these things contradict what scripture says about the good news of the gospel of Christ.

False teachers often speak very eloquently about spiritual things while distorting the Bible. **2 Corinthians 11:13-15 (NIV) says;** [13] **For such men are <u>false apostles, deceitful workmen,</u>**

masquerading as apostles of Christ. [14] **And no wonder, for Satan himself masquerades as an angel of light.** [15] **It is not surprising, then, if his servants masquerade as servants of righteousness. Their end will be what their actions deserve.** They are very skilled at twisting and shaping the words in the Bible to suit their purpose. False apostles usually teach and preach with very little reference to the Bible and seldom use it at all. Paul warns us to watch out for false apostles. In fact, we are taught to test the spirits to see if they are of God.

John the Apostle, shows us in **1 John 4:1-3 (NIV);** [1] **Dear friends, do not believe every spirit, but test the spirits to see whether they are from God, because many false prophets have gone out into the world.** [2] **This is how you can recognize the Spirit of God: Every spirit that acknowledges that Jesus Christ has come in the flesh is from God,** [3] **but every spirit that**

does not acknowledge Jesus is not from God. This is the spirit of the antichrist, which you have heard is coming and even now is already in the world. Apostle John tells us that one of the major tests we can do to see if apostles are false or not is to ask if they believe that Christ Jesus has come in the flesh. Ask them if they believe that Christ Jesus is fully God and fully human because of His birth through the Virgin Mary. In other words, is He fully divine and fully man? False apostles will never admit that Christ Jesus is 100% God and 100% human. They can't admit that because it is against their spirit because they have the spirit of the antichrist. The word antichrist means not for Christ or against Christ. **Revelation 2:2 (NIV) says;** [2] **I know your deeds, your hard work and your perseverance. <u>I know that you cannot tolerate wicked men,</u> that <u>you have tested those who claim to be apostles</u> but are not, and <u>have found them false.</u>** Notice, that scripture says that all apostles were tested in the

False Apostles

book of revelation to see if they were sent by God or not. The testing and authentication of a God sent Apostle isn't based on whether one walked with Christ, was one of the twelve or saw Christ supernaturally. Rather, it is based on whether they preach a Jesus other than the Jesus the Apostles preached according to scripture. Do they teach about a different spirit other then what the Apostles released and taught to the people in the Bible? Do they teach a different gospel from the one that was taught and accepted by the people according to scripture? Finally, do they speak very eloquently, but distort the truth of the word of God? You should test all ministries, churches, speakers and leaders concerning these things. Test everything and always hold on to the truth. Remember, Apostles exist today to bring the church to a place of unity and maturity in the fullness of Christ. Praise God for the wonderful gift we have in our churches today called Apostles!

False Apostles

Chapter Review

1. False apostles exist in today's church.

2. False apostles preach a Jesus other than the Jesus the Apostles preached according to scripture.

3. False apostles release and believe in a different spirit other than who the Apostles released to the people according to scripture in the Bible.

4. False apostles teach a different gospel concerning grace, salvation and resurrection according to the scriptures in the Bible.

5. False apostles might speak very eloquently, but distort the truth of the word of God.

6. We are told to test the spirits to see if the spirit is from God or of the antichrist.

7. The spirit of the antichrist doesn't believe that Christ Jesus is fully divine and fully human.

Appendix

Apostles Mentioned in Scripture and References

1. Christ Jesus (Hebrews 3:1)
2. Simon Peter (Matt. 10:2)
3. Andrew (Matt. 10:2)
4. James the son of Zebedee (Matt. 10:2)
5. John (Matt. 10:2)
6. Philip (Matt. 10:3)
7. Bartholomew (Matt. 10:3)
8. Thomas (Matt. 10:3)
9. Matthew (Matt. 10:3)
10. James the son of Alphaeus (Matt. 10:3)
11. Thaddaeus (Matt. 10:3)
12. Simon the Zealot (Matt. 10:4)
13. Judas Iscariot (Matt. 10:4)
14. Matthias (Acts 1:26)
15. Paul (Gal. 1:1)
16. Barnabas (1 Cor. 9:5-6, Acts 14:4, 14)
17. Andronicus (Rom. 16:7)
18. Junias (Rom. 16:7, also a woman)
19. James, the Lord's half brother (Gal. 1:19)
20. Unknown number of apostles (1 Cor. 15:7)

Epilogue

One of the best ways to experience the complete love of God in your life is for you to give your life to Christ Jesus. Repeat these simple words and it will be a done deal. Repeat the following: Lord Christ Jesus as of this very moment, I accept you as Lord and Savior of my life. I now give my life to you to be fashioned for your purpose and glory. Lord, all of these things that I have said, I truly believe in my heart and have confessed with my mouth to you. I know now that I have received everlasting life based on the work that Christ has done and will continue to do in my life. Lord Christ, thank you for bringing me to this point of my life where I surrender my all to you. It is in the Holy Spirit through Christ Jesus, I say Amen.

Humbly Yours in Christ

Apostle Jamie T. Pleasant

Epilogue

Other Books by Dr. Pleasant

For Speaking Engagements

admin@newzionchristianchurch.org or

678.845.7055

These books can be purchased at any bookstore or online at amazon.com, barnesandnoble.com and many other stores and outlets.

About the Author

About the Author

Apostle Jamie T. Pleasant; Ph.D. is the Chief Executive Pastor and Founder of New Zion Christian Church in Suwanee, Georgia. As a modern day polymath, he holds a bachelor's degree in Physics from Benedict College in Columbia, South Carolina, Marketing Studies from Clemson University and an M.B.A. in Marketing from Clark Atlanta University. On August 13, 1999, Apostle Pleasant achieved a Georgia Tech milestone by becoming the first African American to graduate with a Ph.D. in Business Management in the school's 111 plus year history.

God gave him the vision to establish a Biblically based economic development initiative for New Zion Christian Church. He remains at the pulse of the economic business sector. As a result, Apostle Pleasant is in constant demand to train,

About the Author

speak and teach others at all levels in ministries and the private sector about business and economic development across the country. He has created cutting edge and industry leading ministerial programs in the church such as The Financial Literacy Academy For Youth (FLAFY), where youth from the ages of 13-19 attend 12 week intense classes on financial money management principles. At the end of 12 weeks, they receive a "Personal Finance" certificate of achievement. Other ministries he has pioneered include; The Wealth Builders Investment Club (WBIC), which educates and allows members to actively invest in the stock market, along with the much celebrated Institute of Entrepreneurship (IOE), where participants earn a certificate in Entrepreneurship after three months of comprehensive training in all aspects of starting and owning a successful competitive business. The main goal and purpose of IOE is that each year one of the trained businesses will be awarded

About the Author

up to $10,000 start up money to ensure financial success. The newly added SAT & PSAT prep courses for children ages 9-19 fuels the potential success of all who walk through the doors of New Zion Christian Church.

Apostle Pleasant has met with political officials such as President Clinton and Nelson Mandela. He has delivered the opening prayer for the born again Christian and comedian, Steve Harvey. He has performed marriage ceremonies and counseled numerous celebrated personalities such as Usher Raymond (Confessions Recording Artist), Terri Vaughn (Lavita Jenkins on The Steve Harvey Show), and many others.

He is civically engaged as well. After the Columbine High School shooting, he founded the National School Safety Advocacy Association. His latest foundations include the Young Entrepreneurship Program (YEP) and the African American Consumer Economic Rights (AACER).

About the Author

He has authored seven books, *Prayers That Open Heaven, Capturing and Keeping the Pastor's Heart, Powerful Prayers That Open Heaven, Advertising Principles: How to Effectively Reach African Americans in the 21st Century, Discover a New You: A 21 Day Journey to Uncovering Your Uniqueness, From My Heart To Yours: Love Letters From A Loving Father and Today's Apostle: Servants of God, Leading His People towards Unity.*

Apostle Pleasant is the husband of Kimberly Pleasant (whom he loves dearly) and the proud father of three children: Christian, Zion and Nacara.

FINI

www.ingramcontent.com/pod-product-compliance
Lightning Source LLC
Chambersburg PA
CBHW032135090426
42743CB00007B/600